COLOURS

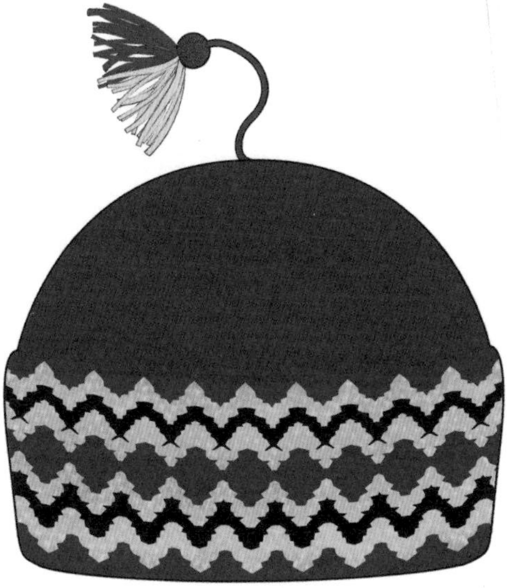

ILLUSTRATED BY

Haana-SikSik Lavallee

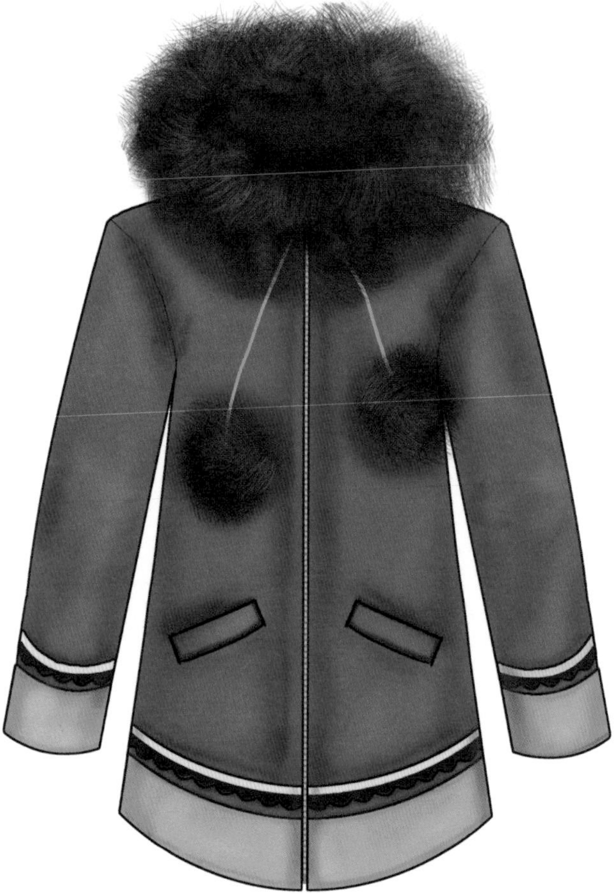

blue

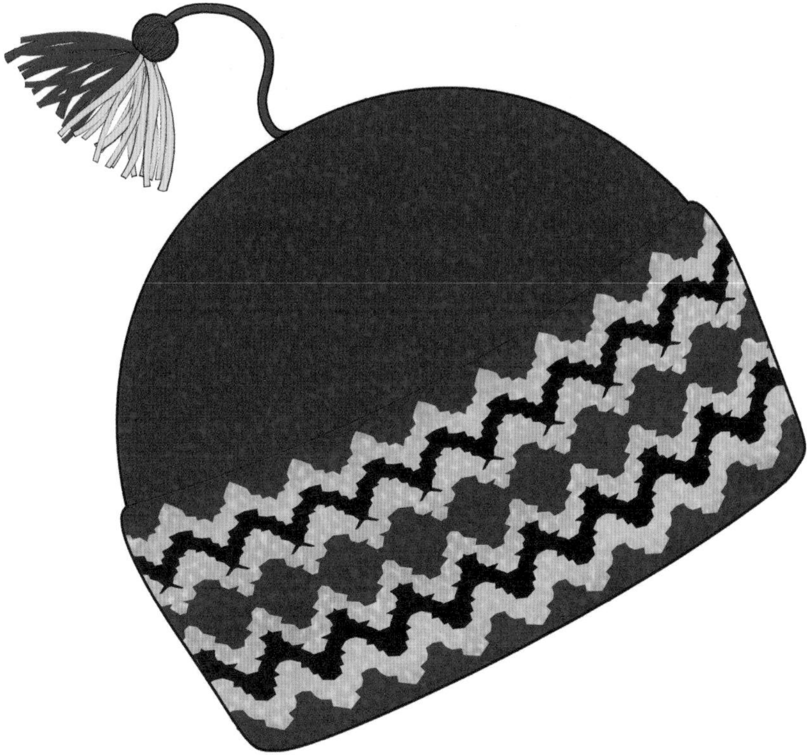

red

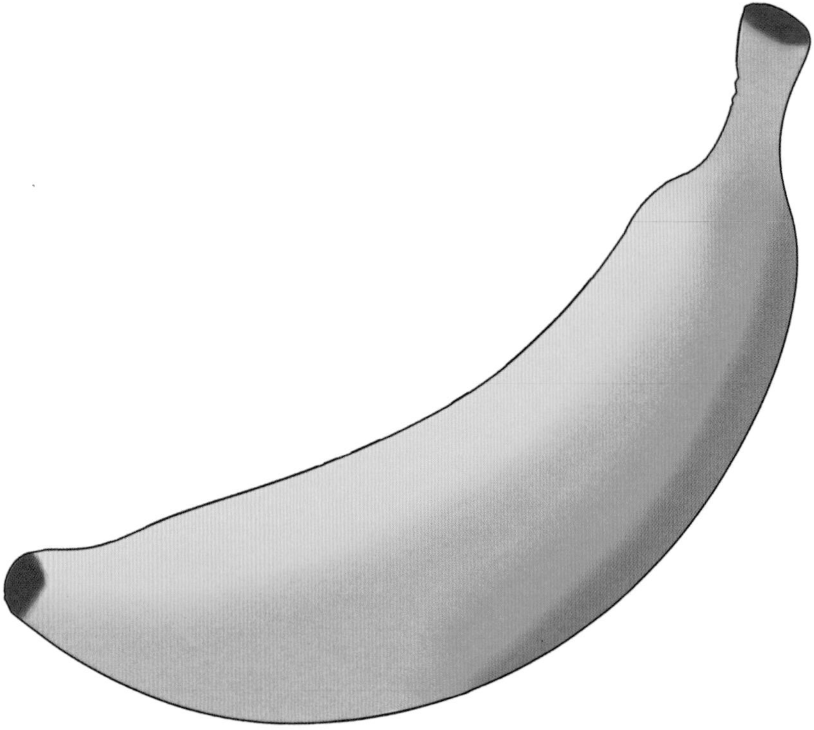

yellow

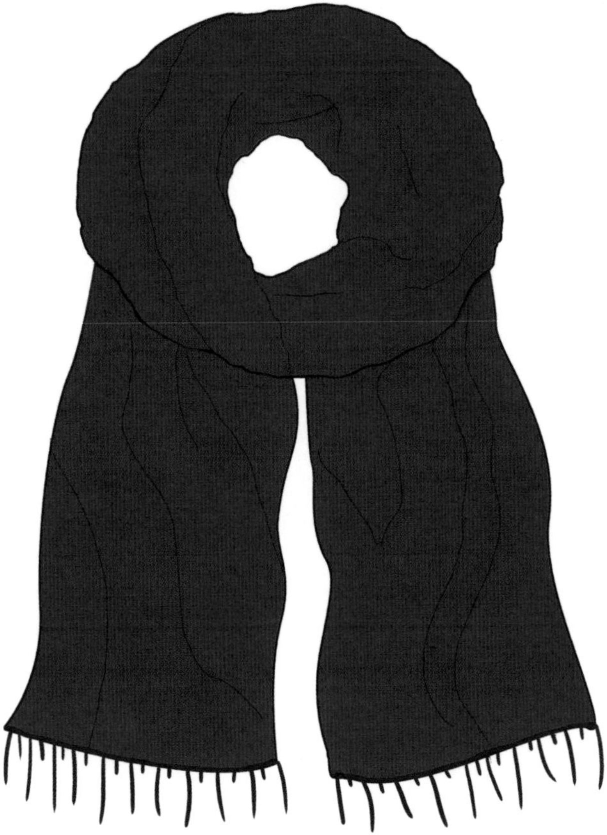

purple

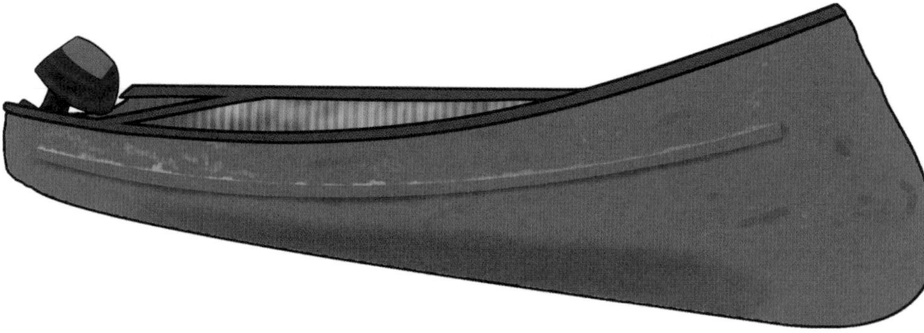

green

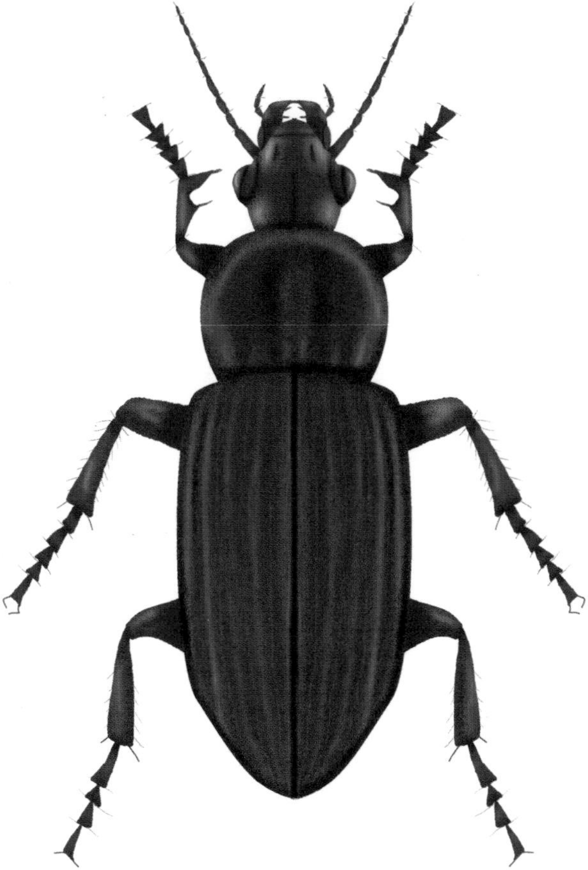

black

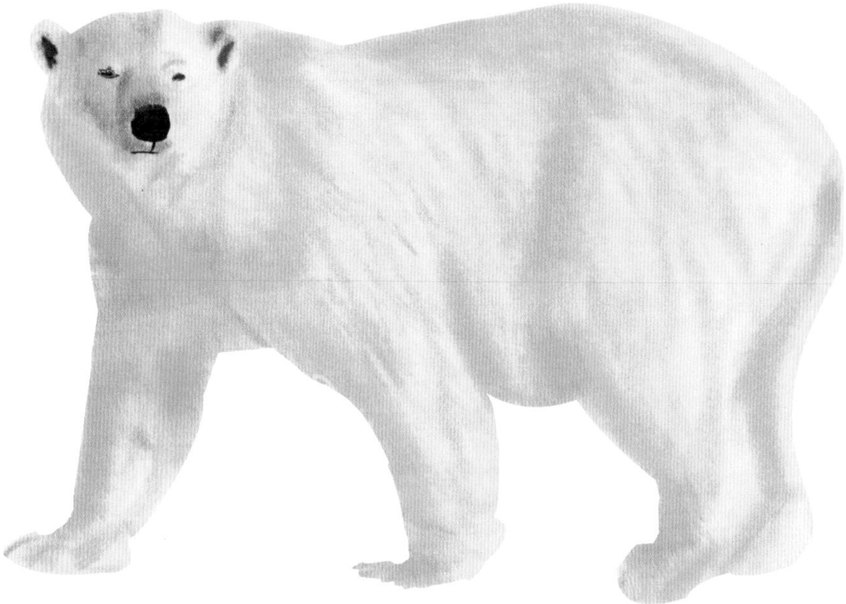

white

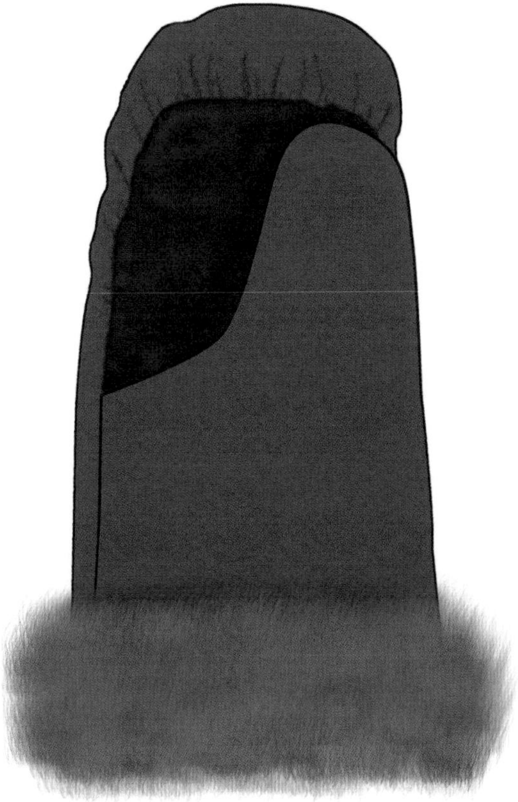

brown

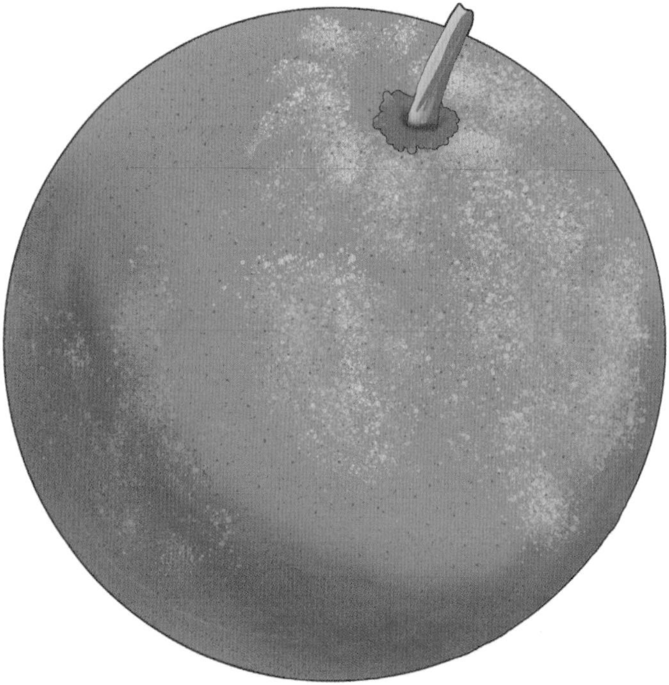

orange

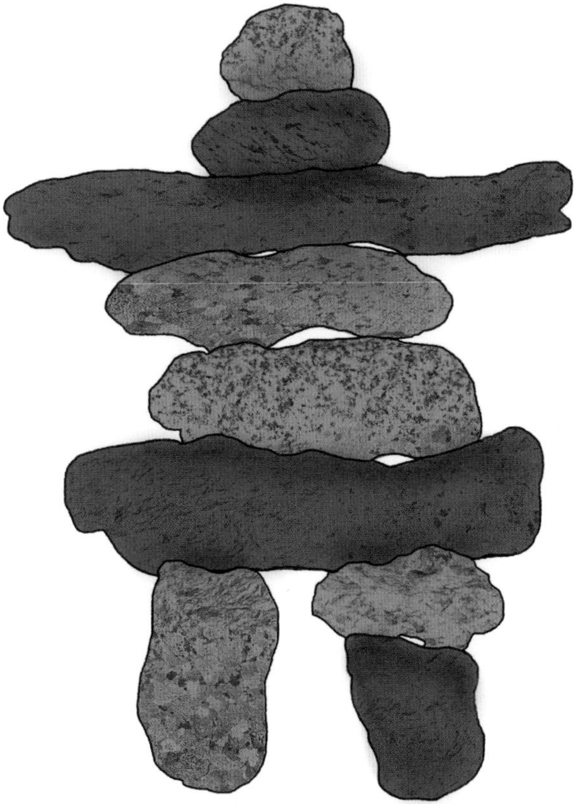

grey

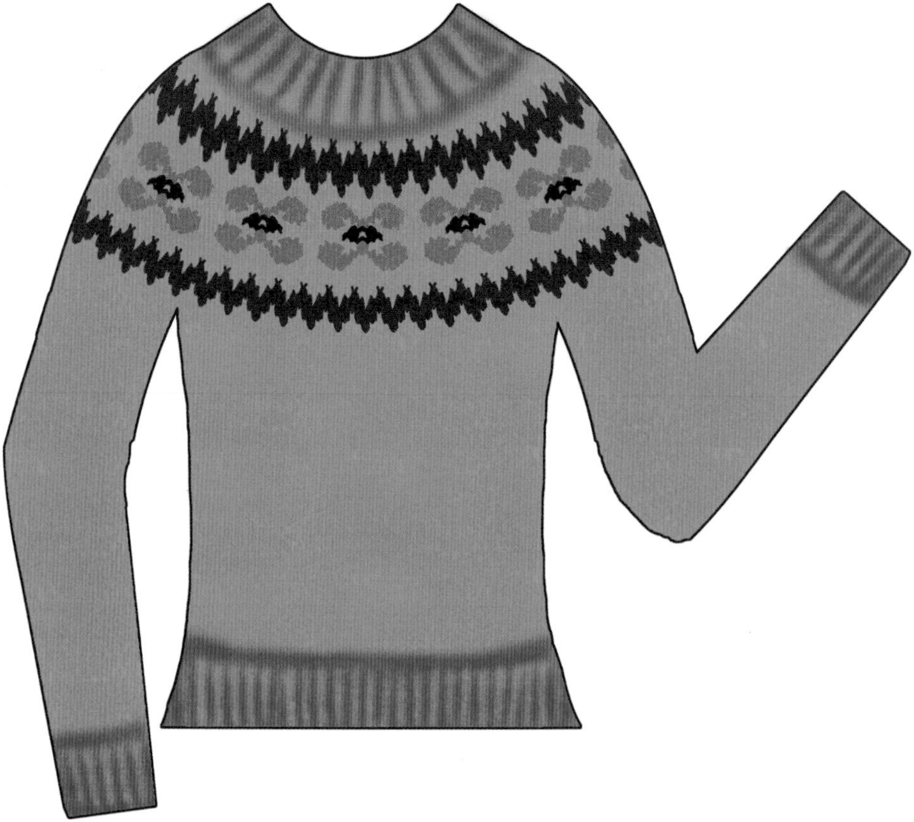

pink